Breathe It!

Quick Breathing Hacks for Kids to Calm, Focus, and Energize

Little C Books

Corbett Shwom

Note to Parents and Caregivers

This book helps your child discover the power of their breath, a simple, practical way to feel calm, focused, and full of energy. Each breathing technique is kid-friendly, easy to follow, and designed to build confidence, resilience, and emotional strength.

Learning to breathe on purpose is a skill kids can use for life. It helps them manage big feelings, find focus, and recharge whether at school, at home, or on the go.

Most techniques include gentle counting or timed breaths for structure, making them easy to follow and supporting mindfulness too.

These exercises work anytime, anywhere, and they are great for grown-ups as well. Try them yourself and share the calm, focus, and energy with your child.

Published by Worry House Press
First Edition
Printed in the United States of America

www.corbettshwom.com

To all the amazing kids out there, this book is for you. Life can get a bit crazy sometimes, but that's okay. No matter what's happening around you, your breath can help you feel calm, focused, and full of energy. We all want to feel strong, steady, and ready. Remember, you can always take a moment for yourself. Breathe in, breathe out, and let your superpower shine!

Hi, I'm Little C, your guide to the superpower of breathwork!
You might remember me from the other Little C books, but this time it's all about using your breath to help you feel calm, focused, or full of energy.

Did you know you can change how you feel just by changing how you breathe?
Go ahead, try it now. Breathe in through your nose for four seconds, then out through your mouth for four seconds. Feels good, right? 😊

That's breathwork! It simply means using your breath on purpose to help your body and mind feel better.

Here's the best part. You can use your breath anytime, anywhere.
Before a test? When you're upset? When you need a boost?
Whenever you need it, **Breathe It!**

- 🔵 Need to feel calm? *Breathe It!*
- 🟡 Need to focus? *Breathe It!*
- 🟠 Need more energy? *Breathe It!*

Each page shows a quick breathing hack and an example of when I use it.
You'll see **Try It!** before each breath. Read it first, then give it a go!
Look for **C's Tip** to make each hack even better.

Some breaths work best sitting, some standing, some lying down, and some while you move. The pictures show one way but make each hack your own.

I even get help from my friends **Little A** and **Little E**. Each demonstrates one special technique.

Just remember to breathe gently and never force it.
If you ever feel dizzy or uncomfortable, stop and return to your normal breathing.

Are you ready? Turn the page and let's explore your new superpower.
Need calm, focus, or energy? **Breathe It!**

○ Calm Breathing
Try these hacks to feel relaxed and centered!

Ocean Wave
A flowing breath to help you relax.

Long Exhale
A slow breath to steady your body.

Shoulder Release
A gentle breath and shoulder drop to let go.

Cloud Breath
A soft breath to float your worries away.

Candle Breath
A quiet breath to steady your nerves.

○ Ocean Wave

A flowing breath that moves like ocean waves to help you relax.

👉 **Try It!**

1. Sit, stand, or lie down, whatever feels best.
2. With your mouth closed, breathe in slowly through your nose for 4 seconds, making a soft "ha" sound in your throat.
3. Breathe out through your nose until your belly is empty, making your "ha" sound a little louder.
4. Repeat three times, imagining your breath like ocean waves.

💡 **C's Tip**

Hand on your belly as you breathe out to feel it empty and to make a 'ha' sound, it's like fogging a window but with your nose.

○ Long Exhale

A slow breath to help your body feel steady and still.

👉 **Try It!**

1. Sit, stand, or lie down, whatever feels best.
2. Breathe in deeply through your nose for 4 seconds.
3. Breathe out slowly through your mouth for 8 seconds.
4. Place a hand on your belly as you breathe out to feel it empty.
5. Repeat three times, keeping your breath steady and smooth.

💡 **C's Tip**

If 4 in and 8 out feels too long, try 2 in and 4 out. Just keep the breath out twice as long as the breath in.

⊙ Shoulder Release

A gentle breath and shoulder drop to help you let go and relax.

👉**Try It!**
1. Sit, stand, or lie down, whatever feels best.
2. Breathe in slowly through your nose for 4 seconds as you shrug your shoulders up toward your ears.
3. Breathe out slowly through your mouth for 4 seconds as you drop your shoulders and relax.
4. Repeat three times, letting go of your worries one breath at a time.

💡 **C's Tip**
Imagine you're dropping a heavy backpack with each breath out.

⭕ Cloud Breath

A soft breath that helps your worries float away.

👉**Try It!**
1. Sit, stand, or lie down, whatever feels best.
2. Breathe in slowly through your nose for 4 seconds, feel your body get light like a cloud.
3. Breathe out slowly through your mouth for 4 seconds, like you're gently blowing a cloud across the sky.
4. Repeat three times, feeling lighter with each breath.

💡 **C's Tip**
  As you breathe out, let your worries float away with the clouds.

○ Candle Breath
A quiet breath to steady your mind and nerves.

👉**Try It!**
1. Sit, stand, or lie down, whatever feels best.
2. Breathe in slowly through your nose for 4 seconds.
3. Breathe out gently through your mouth, imagining a candle flame that moves but doesn't go out.
4. Place a hand on your belly as you breathe out to feel it empty.
5. Repeat three times, keeping your breath slow and smooth.

💡 **C's Tip**
Don't blow out the flame, it's not a birthday candle!

Focus Breathing

Try these hacks to feel alert and ready to act!

Three Slow Breaths
A slow breath you take three times to reset.

Box Breathing
An even breath you trace to feel in control.

Mindful Breathing
A quiet breath to stay right here, right now.

Step Breath
A rhythmic breath to stay balanced.

Counting Breaths
A measured breath to keep your mind on track.

⬤ Three Slow Breaths

A slow breath you take three times to reset and feel ready.

👉 Try It!

1. Stand or sit tall, whatever feels best.
2. Breathe in slowly through your nose for 3 seconds.
3. Breathe out slowly through your mouth for 3 seconds.
4. That's one full breath. Each one helps you reset and refocus.
5. Repeat two more times for a total of three slow breaths.

💡 A's Tip

Keep your eyes on one thing while taking full breaths to boost your focus even more (and remember to blink!).

● Box Breathing

An even breath you trace like a box in your mind to feel in control.

👉 **Try It!**
1. Stand or sit tall, whatever feels best.
2. Breathe in through nose for 4 seconds, draw one side of the box.(1)
3. Hold your breath for 4 seconds, draw the top.(2)
4. Breathe out through mouth for 4 seconds, draw the other side.(3)
5. Hold your breath again for 4 seconds, finish the box!(4)
6. Repeat three times. Keep each breath smooth and steady.

💡 **C's Tip**
   Imagine a glowing box in the air. You can trace it with your finger, eyes, or in your mind to stay focused.

● Mindful Breathing

A quiet breath that helps your mind stay right here, right now.

👉Try It!

1. Stand or sit tall, whatever feels best.
2. Breathe in slowly through your nose, feel your belly rise like a balloon.
3. Breathe out slowly through your nose, let the balloon gently empty.
4. Repeat three times, imagining your breath filling and emptying the balloon.

💡 C's Tip

If your mind starts to wander, that's okay! Gently bring your focus back to your breath and start again.

● Step Breath

A rhythmic breath you match with your steps to feel balanced.

👉 **Try It!**

1. Walk slowly in a safe place.
2. Breathe in through your nose as you take three steps.
3. Breathe out through your mouth as you take three more steps.
4. Keep matching your breath with your steps, in 3, out 3.
5. Do this for a little while until you feel steady and focused.

💡 **C's Tip**

If you prefer not to walk, just march softly in place and match your breath to your steps.

○ Counting Breaths

A measured breath you count to keep your mind on track.

👉 **Try It!**

1. Stand or sit tall, whatever feels best.
2. Take a full breath in through your nose and count "1" in your head.
3. Breathe out slowly through your nose and count "2."
4. Keep going, count "3" as you breathe in, "4" as you breathe out.
5. Continue counting your breaths until you reach "10."

💡 *C's Tip*

If counting to "10" feels too long or short, count to what feels right. If you lose count, just start again at "1."

Energize Breathing
Try these hacks to feel awake and ready to move!

Humming Breath
A buzzing breath to boost your mood.

Strong Breath
A big breath to feel bold and ready.

Balloon Breath
A growing breath to fill your body with energy.

Refresh Breath
A cool breath to shake off tired feelings.

Quick Sniff
A fast breath to help you wake up.

Humming Breath

A buzzing breath to wake you up and boost your mood.

👉 **Try It!**

1. Stand or sit tall, whatever feels best.
2. Take a big breath in through your nose for 4 seconds, filling your belly with air.
3. Breathe out slowly through your nose for 4 seconds, making a soft "mmm" sound like a humming bee.
4. Repeat three times for a quick energy boost.

💡 **C's Tip**

Imagine a busy bee humming! The louder you hum, the more you'll feel the buzz in your chest.

🟠 Strong Breath

A big breath to help you feel bold and ready for action.

👉 **Try It!**

1. Stand or sit tall, whatever feels best.
2. Take a big breath in through your nose for 4 seconds, filling your belly and chest.
3. Breathe out strongly through your mouth, like you're blowing away nervous feelings.
4. Repeat three times, feeling your confidence grow!

💡 **C's Tip**

For an extra boost, raise your arms as you breathe in and lower them as you breathe out.

⬤ Balloon Breath

A growing breath to fill your body with fresh energy.

👉 **Try It!**

1. Stand or sit tall, whatever feels best.
2. Breathe in through your nose for 3 seconds, filling your belly like a big balloon.
3. Breathe out slowly through your mouth, letting it gently empty.
4. Repeat three times and get ready to dance like you're at your favorite concert!

💡 **E's Tip**

You can never have enough friendship bracelets. ❤️

● Refresh Breath

A cool breath to help you shake off tired feelings.

👉 Try It!

1. Purse your lips like you're sipping through a straw.
2. Breathe in cool air through your mouth for 3 seconds, like a gentle breeze.
3. Breathe out slowly through your nose for 4 seconds, feeling the cool energy spread through your body.
4. Repeat three times to feel awake and ready to go!

💡 C's Tip

Imagine you're sipping a cool drink on a hot day, it makes the breath feel even more refreshing.

⬤ Quick Sniff

A fast breath to help you wake up and feel alert.

👉 Try It!

1. Stand or sit tall, whatever feels best.
2. Take a quick sniff in through your nose for 1 second, filling your belly with air.
3. Breathe out slowly through your nose for 4 seconds, letting your body relax.
4. Repeat three times to feel more awake and energized.

💡 C's Tip

Try it with a smile! A quick sniff and a smile can wake you up even faster.

Author's Note

Thanks for joining Little C on this journey into the power of breathwork. Who knew we had this superpower all along? Practicing breathwork can help you feel strong, confident, brave, even happy.

Listen to your body and take care of yourself as you try each technique. Every breath in this book is here to help you. Notice which ones feel good and make them your own. Go slower or faster, quieter or bigger. It's totally up to you!

The best part? You can use most of these anytime, anywhere, and no one will even notice. And even if they do, who cares? You're taking care of you, and that's awesome!

Keep practicing, keep growing, and enjoy your breathing superpower every day, just like Little C. And remember, **Whenever you need it, Breathe It! ♥**

Other Titles by Corbett Shwom

Worry Thoughts
A Story to Help Children Manage Worries and Anxious Thoughts

Worry Habits
A Story to Help Children Better Understand and Manage OCD

Worry Shy
A Story to Help Children Better Understand and Manage Social Anxiety

Be It! Act It!
An Alphabet of Positive Emotions and Feelings

www.ingramcontent.com/pod-product-compliance
Lightning Source LLC
Chambersburg PA
CBHW041557040426

42447CB00002B/199